I0422562

GET UP, GET OUT, AND VOLUNTEER!

With love and dedication,

to my wife, Leslie, and my children, Todd and Nora.

GET UP, GET OUT, AND VOLUNTEER!

A simple book that will change your life.

Dale Wallenius

GET UP, GET OUT, AND VOLUNTEER!
A SIMPLE BOOK THAT WILL CHANGE YOUR LIFE.

Copyright © 2003, 2019 Dale Wallenius.

All rights reserved. No part of this book may be used or reproduced by any means, graphic, electronic, or mechanical, including photocopying, recording, taping or by any information storage retrieval system without the written permission of the author except in the case of brief quotations embodied in critical articles and reviews.

iUniverse books may be ordered through booksellers or by contacting:

iUniverse
1663 Liberty Drive
Bloomington, IN 47403
www.iuniverse.com
1-800-Authors (1-800-288-4677)

Because of the dynamic nature of the Internet, any web addresses or links contained in this book may have changed since publication and may no longer be valid. The views expressed in this work are solely those of the author and do not necessarily reflect the views of the publisher, and the publisher hereby disclaims any responsibility for them.

ISBN: 978-0-5952-9343-8 (sc)

Print information available on the last page.

iUniverse rev. date: 05/22/2019

CONTENTS

▼

CHAPTER 1

▼

THE MOST ENRICHING JOB YOU'LL EVER HAVE

(IT'S NOT ABOUT THE MONEY, HONEY)

"No person was ever honored for what he received. Honor has been rewarded for what he gave."
—Calvin Coolidge

Everything I ever needed to know about fatherhood, I learned in fundraising. Okay, that statement may be somewhat of an exaggeration. But there is some truth to it, as well. Let me explain.

While there are some parents out there who dare to hope that their kids merely "stay out of trouble," as a father of two, I have far higher expectations. My fondest hope is that my children will earn reputations for their altruism, compassion, fortitude, generosity of spirit, self-respect and respect for others; that their lifetimes will be blessed with lasting friendships and a sense of belonging; that when they leave this planet, it be with the inner peace that comes from knowing they have helped to make it a better place for their fellow man. Who among us doesn't want this for their children—for ourselves?

Well, thanks to over two decades' worth of experience in the fundraising business, I know there is a type of hands-on training that can make these wishes a reality—not just for me and for my kids, but for you and for yours, as well. By hands-on training, I refer to none other than the simple act of volunteerism. When we as human beings give of our time, when we give of our talents, when we give of ourselves, these things come to us.

> *"I believe to the depth of my heart that a teenager who has spent a few hours a week helping a younger child learn to read, or spent a few hours at a hospice helping an older person reach the end of their life in dignity, is a changed person."*
> —**General Colin L. Powell**

Throughout my career, I have had the pleasure of dealing with countless volunteers of varying interests, ages, and walks of life. Personal conversations I have had with them have led me to place great stock in the truism that "what you give you get back tenfold."

Recently, in an attempt to find out what it is that motivates people to volunteer, I surveyed some 350 volunteers from all across the nation. Without fail, my survey respondents alluded to one of five very specific motivations for volunteering:

> ➤ a desire to "help others"
> ➤ a sense of duty to "give back to the community"
> ➤ personal experiences and rewards
> ➤ the wish to connect with people
> ➤ a desire to "make a difference"

Do any of these motivations strike a chord in you? If so, you might be interested to know that the survey respondents reported that they found overwhelming fulfillment through their volunteer endeavors. But don't take my word for it. Instead, read for yourself what they had to say about the personal rewards of volunteerism in the following pages. You'll also find some interesting statistics on volunteerism in America and some famous quotes on community service that I think are worth hearing again and again.

I know the reason you picked up this book is that you're feeling the pull to contribute your unique talents and energies to a worthy cause. Whether that cause is to feed the hungry, comfort the sick, read to the blind, promote the arts, find loving homes for ownerless pets, plant a tree, or any of the thousands of other activities awaiting your personal attention, I hope this book serves to reinforce that positive impulse. The world at large stands to benefit, and so do you! Remember:

"We learn the inner secret of happiness when we learn to direct our inner drives, our interest and attention to something outside ourselves."

—Ethel Percy Andrus

What's that you say? Don't know where to begin? Let me assure you that there is a need for all types of volunteer assistance out there. Special training is usually not a prerequisite. If you have goodwill in your heart, a smile on your face, and precious time you can share, that's all it takes to make a difference in the life of someone in need.

"I was raised in an orphanage, 5 to 16 years of age. In those days, I was referred to as a 'Ward of the Court,' i.e., parents divorced and my mother could not support me. Now in my 'late life' (80 years old) I've decided to complete full circle and take care of those in need as I was taken care of at an early age. I feel compassion for those in need."

—Eugene Weith
Second Harvest Food Bank,
Community Health Care Center,
Meditation Center,
Kiwanis-Kids Programs,
Savannah, Georgia

Of course, if you are hoping to gain experience in a particular area, many volunteer organizations are delighted to provide special training. That's something to consider if you're one of those people who thrives on the stimulation of learning new things. Likewise, if you have a special hobby or area of expertise, you may find certain organizations out there that can really put your skills to good use.

"You can be a spectator or a participant. I choose the latter because I've had several people help me through things in life and it's my way to give back."

—Liana Collalti
Freeport Memorial Hospital,
Freeport, Illinois

For instance, nature lovers can help maintain hiking trails at a national park, or perhaps work with a wildlife protection agency to help track endangered species. Photo buffs can use their skills to document fundraising events or create child safety IDs. Editors can lend their proofing eyes to non-profit newsletters and publications.

> *"I volunteer so that our youth won't have to go shortchanged. Our children are our future, and by giving a little of my own time, I can be a part of that future. A man or a woman can donate money so many will not have to go without food or a place to live, but I feel the true gift is in giving one's own time and sharing one's own experience, strength and hopes for the future."*
>
> —David Alexander
> Waikiki Aquarium,
> University of Hawaii,
> Honolulu, Hawaii

If it hadn't occurred to you before, I hope it is dawning on you now that when you seek out the right activity and an organization you are truly passionate about, volunteering can be loads of fun!

> *"I volunteer because I know there are many needs in the community for which there is inadequate or no funding, and many persons have to work and care for families, so they do not have time to donate. I'm retired with an adequate income, so I have the time. Therefore, I should volunteer. Besides, I enjoy it. It's fun to do what one likes to do rather than what one has to do."*
>
> —Anita Mitchell
> Meals on Wheels,
> Darwin D. Martin House,
> Graycliff,
> Kenmore Presbyterian Church,
> Library-Tonawanda,
> Buffalo Derby,
> Kenmore, New York

The many thousands of volunteer jobs out there are as varied and interesting as the personalities of the volunteers who will one day fill them. In the back of this book is a list of organizations that can help you find the most mentally, emotionally, and spiritually fulfilling volunteer opportunity for you.

So what are you waiting for? As a father, as a fundraiser, as a friend, and as a fellow American, I urge you to follow your instinct to get up, get out, and volunteer!

CHAPTER 2

▼

HELP OTHERS, HELP YOURSELF

"The one who dreamed the universe loved circles and created every-thing with such beautiful incompletion that we need the others to complete the circles of identity, belonging, and creativity."
—John O'Donohue

According to a recent survey conducted by the Bureau of Labor Statistics, about 25 percent of Americans volunteer annually. That simply isn't good enough. The number should be 100 percent! America is built on a tradition of volunteerism. Did you know our War of Independence was fought and won by an army of volunteer soldiers? And it was the anti-slavery movement of the Civil War era that brought forth one of the most crucial and daring volunteer efforts of our history—the Underground Railroad.

From the community barn raisings of pioneer days to the houses being built by Habitat for Humanity today, that same volunteer spirit continues to make our country great. So why don't more people roll up their sleeves and do their part to keep the American tradition of volunteerism alive and well?

We can all come up with dozens of reasons for sabotaging our natural instinct to do good. These reasons may be valid, but if we look a little deeper, we'll discover they have workable solutions.

"Everyone should be obligated to give back something to their community…if everyone did just one thing to make this a better world, just think what we will have accomplished."

—Carl Zaar
St. John Antida High School,
Milwaukee, Wisconsin

If you are like many working adults, the idea of volunteering may seem out of the question due to the enormous demands already on your time. Conceptually, you may like the idea, but with expectations to meet both at the workplace and at home, you worry that something or someone along the way—a colleague, a child, a spouse, or an elderly parent, perhaps—may be shortchanged. The fact of the matter is, if you ignore that inner voice that's telling you to get out there and give of yourself, the person who ends up getting shortchanged just might be you!

"Twenty years from now you will be more disappointed by the things that you didn't do than by the ones you did do."

—Mark Twain

"My parents stressed that people should take advantage of community benefits, i.e., educational opportunities, employment, the cultural arts…but remember to give back some of their time, talent and treasures. Over the years, I have used the U.S. Jaycees' creed as my personal guiding light. The last line reads:'…and service to humanity is the best work of life.'"

—B. Vann Johnson
Ordinary People…Extraordinary Needs,
HIV/AIDS Ministry of York County,
Council of Churches,
York, Pennsylvania

"My biggest reward in volunteering is being able to look myself in the mirror at the end of the day and know that I've given…and as a result, I've also received."

—David Oscar Ocanas
Don Bosco Technical Institute,
Alumni Association,
Rosemead, California

"I have been greatly blessed in life with health, happiness, and a wonderful family. I feel that my helping others in some way repays my debt. I feel that in giving, we receive."

—Dollie Galbraith
Hospice of the Bluegrass,
Lexington, Kentucky

If you view volunteering solely as an independent enterprise, think again! For many, it's a family affair. Spending time together working toward a common goal often brings families closer together, and I can think of no better way to instill all the right values in your children.

"I volunteer to show my daughters how they can assist and make an impact on other people's lives—to give back."

—Lois Mitchell
Girl Scouts,
Montecito Union School,
Transition House,
Santa Barbara, California

"I have been very fortunate in life and feel it is my responsibility to 'give back' to our community. I also believe it sets a good example for my children."

—Virginia Ranger
Morristown Memorial Hospital,
Family Service,
Morristown, New Jersey

"I am setting an example for my children so that they can see the value of giving time, not just money. The benefits far outweigh the time and energy used."

—Martha Clark
Maryland Agricultural Education Foundation,
Soil Conservation District,
Maryland Agricultural Commission, Farm Bureau,
Maryland

DID YOU KNOW?

Youth who volunteer are three times more likely to volunteer as adults (Independent Sector/Gallup, 1996). Check out some of the opportunities listed on www.familycares.org, where you'll find information geared specifically toward volunteerism for older adults, youth, and families.

> *"I am a professional volunteer, having begun my volunteer work as a teenager working in a local hospital during World War II, when I was in high school. My mother taught me at an early age that it was important to share what you have with others, particularly the less fortunate. I have carried this forward throughout my adult life wherever I have lived."*
>
> —Nancy Dunne
> Anna Maria Island Community Center,
> Anna Maria, Florida

> **"If every American donated five hours a week, it would equal the labor of 20 million full-time volunteers."**
> **—Whoopi Goldberg**

If a hectic work schedule is preventing you from volunteering, you aren't alone. Some people's schedules are so erratic, they will never be able to take on such awesome responsibilities as teaching adults to read or mentoring children. These types of commitments are more rewarding than you can imagine, but they do require considerable amounts of time and effort.

It is better to be realistic about your limitations than to go around making promises you won't be able to keep. If you are serious about wanting to make a difference, you should know that there are short-term volunteer opportunities out there that may be better suited to your lifestyle. If all you can give is a couple of hours every third Sunday of the month, you'll get no arguments here. The important thing is that you give what you can.

> *"I can't really describe my feelings other than to say that it feels 'right.' I don't do it out of some sort of moral or religious or civic obligation—it just feel like what I need to do."*
>
> —Rodney Waters
> Interfaith Ministries for Greater Houston,
> Houston, Texas

"Volunteering makes me feel like I'm doing the right thing. It connects me to my community and myself. It makes me feel lucky. I get to hear people's amazing stories, witness their healing, and color with them. (I'm much better at coloring since I started volunteering!) It lets me see what a difference people can make in each other's lives."

—Rayna Krohn
California Pacific Medical Center,
San Francisco, California

Returning for a moment to the subject of work, here's a thought for those of you who occupy the upper rungs of the corporate ladder. Why not share the rewards of volunteerism with your employees? Investigate the possibility of incorporating community service into the company mission statement, and not only will your employees and all the people they help thank you, but so will your CEO. There is a growing trend in corporate America to use employee volunteerism as a method for enhancing teamwork skills. (It doesn't do the company's reputation any harm, either.)

"I believe we all have a responsibility to give back to others/community, since we have been blessed with so much ourselves. I have a great need and desire to give back."

—Mark Conzeminis
Saint Mary's Youth Ministry,
Sioux Falls, South Dakota

DID YOU KNOW?

In a recent poll, some 68 percent of respondents agreed that corporate volunteer programs helped retain valued employees, and 58 percent said they felt employee volunteering led to increased productivity. (SOURCE: volunteercenter.org, February 2003.)

"Volunteering is a very important part of giving back to society. It has been my dream to see a volunteer program established at the museum. My dream has come true! I know that I am giving of myself to an organization that has given so much to me. Some things in life are priceless; to me that's what volunteering is—priceless—an ultimate gift back to the world."

—Suzi Bellville-Fisher
Motorcycle Hall of Fame Museum,
Pickerington, Ohio

If you can't "get out" to do your volunteering for whatever reason, be it a crazy work schedule, transportation problems, or physical disability, you can still do your part to give back to the community if you have access to a personal computer and an Internet connection. In case you haven't heard, there is a fast-growing trend out there known as "virtual volunteering." This is something that allows people to participate in volunteer projects without ever having to leave the comfort of their own homes.

> *"I volunteer for the reason of helping those in need. It gives me pleasure to help others that are suffering from a disease they have no control of."*
>
> —Shirley Joseph
> Sickle Cell Foundation,
> West Palm Beach, Florida

Some "online volunteers" mentor latchkey kids via e-mail or instant messaging; others conduct "online visitations" with hospital patients or rest home residents; and still others use their design, writing, or editing skills to create newsletters or Websites for non-profit organizations. As far as I'm concerned, the limitless potential for good work that can be accomplished online more than makes up for all that annoying spam I find in my e-mail inbox!

> *"I believe our greatest emotional, mental, and spiritual needs are met by focusing on the welfare of others."*
>
> —Sherri Mills
> Makena Children's Foundation,
> Birmingham, Alabama

> *"With volunteering, I have the opportunity to meet adults and children, and through the interactivity with them, I feel I grow in my understanding of others. With volunteer work, I can give of myself in helping others and help the organizations that depend upon volunteers to help the community."*
>
> —Ruth Gates
> Morris Performing Arts Center,
> South Bend, Indiana

Now that we've addressed ways to overcome the various barriers to volunteerism, let's talk about some common fears and misapprehensions you may have. First off, you needn't be a stand-up comedian or even wildly extroverted by nature to make a difference in the lives of those in need. And if you do happen to be an introvert, that doesn't mean you should avoid those activities that involve heavy one-on-one communication. Your first instinct might be to enlist your services in the less people-oriented roles, but I encourage you to step outside the box! When we direct our focus outside of ourselves and extend a helping hand to others, it reminds us who we truly are and allows us to fully experience authentic, inner happiness.

> *"I gain accomplishment and satisfaction in helping others. Knowing that I can make a positive contribution to someone makes me very thankful for the things I have and puts life into perspective."*
> —Jean Lampe
> American Red Cross,
> Rockville, Maryland

> *"I feel great when assisting others less fortunate than myself. It provides me with an exhilarating, existential feeling of self-worth."*
> —Shelby Roberts
> Lighthouse of Oakland County,
> Pontiac, Michigan

> **"We are each of us angels with only one wing. And we can only fly embracing each other."**
> **—Luciano de Crescenzo**

It doesn't matter how much or how little life experience you have. By reaching out to others, you'll gain a deeper perspective on the world around you and better understand your place in it. Whether you're a senior citizen or a senior in high school, there's a multitude of reasons to make volunteering an important dimension of your life. One that applies to both groups is this: Volunteering gives you the chance to "get outside your own head."

> *"Being aware of the plight of others is always a value in keeping my own problems in perspective."*
> —Kay Sims
> Ronald McDonald House,
> Palo Alto, California

"I have a sense of contributing to something bigger than me and making the community a better place to live."
　　　　　　　　　　　　　　　　　　—Jim Eskin
　　　　　　　　　　　　　　　　Goodwill Industries,
　　　　　　　　　　　　　　　　San Antonio, Texas

At every age, we can fall into the trap of over-dramatizing the events of our daily existence. We worry about things like "keeping up with the Joneses," and "he said, she said." When we take a moment to stop and consider the real life problems other members of our communities face on a daily basis—homelessness, hunger, and disability—we come to understand that these other things we obsess over are beneath us. Simply put, volunteering helps us put things in their proper perspective.

"I get the personal satisfaction of knowing I am helping others while keeping my mind active and busy. I feel good about myself knowing I have helped someone have a better day. I take a lot of pride in my work and I know I have [helped] and can help a lot of people."
　　　　　　　　　　　　　　　　　　—Ronald Gordon
　　　　　　　　　　　　　　Senior Citizens East, AARP,
　　　　　　　　　　　　Tax Counseling for the Elderly,
　　　　　　　　　　　　　Kentucky Refugee Ministry,
　　　　　　　　　　　　　　　　　Salvation Army,
　　　　　　　　　　　　Actors Theater of Louisville,
　　　　　　　　　　　　　　　Louisville, Kentucky

"I get a great feeling of satisfaction and accomplishment. I love knowing that what I've created has had a positive impact on not only the people around me, but on people I have never met and will never know. It's my own sort of immortality."
　　　　　　　　　　　　　　　　　　—Pamela Lopez
　　　　　　　　　　　　Ventura County Arts Council,
　　　　　　　　　Westlake Hills Elementary School,
　　　　　　　　　　　Westlake Village, California

"I searched to discover something that would give meaning to a life that was in chaos, crises, and severely damaged. In a brainstorming session with my wife, brother, and sister-in-law, I determined that I should spend the rest of my life doing full time what I had only done part time in the past. That is, to help others."

—Stanley Lewy
Thresholds,
Chicago, Illinois

In order for the golden years to be just that, it is important that we hold on tight to that zest for life. Sometimes that's easier said than done. I've met folks who look forward to retirement all their lives only to find themselves bored and unhappy when it finally arrives. Then they start volunteering, and the immense satisfaction they feel when they start devoting their efforts to helping others is life changing.

"After retirement, I decided that my love of engineering could be used to give something back to the profession by getting young people interested in the basics of the sciences. There is an intangible reward that can best be expressed as pride. This type of reward is exponentially related to what you put into giving…volunteering is fundamentally an act of giving."

—Edward Mallonen
Urban Day School,
Milwaukee, Wisconsin

Sometimes we lose sight of the fact that it's love, not money, that makes the world go 'round. Improving the lives of those around you by giving of your time and talents can bring so much more satisfaction than merely contributing to the bottom line of a big corporation.

"I volunteer to remain physically and mentally active and to give back for so many blessings my family has received."

—Barbara Loux
Manna Food Pantry,
Pensacola, Florida

"Don't just count your years, make your years count."

—Ernest Meyers

"A graceful and honorable old age is the childhood of immortality."
—Pindar

High school students: Here's a tip for you. No matter what your post-graduation plans may be, you'll be doing yourself a tremendous favor if you start your volunteer career without further delay. Nothing is more impressive on a young person's resume or college application than a track record of community service. Employers like giving jobs to trustworthy people who have demonstrated a commitment to giving back to the community and helping others. The same goes for college boards. They are more likely to admit—even provide scholarships—to applicants with glowing letters of recommendation from business people and community leaders.

But the biggest benefit of all? You just don't know how good it's going to feel to shift your focus off the daily grind and onto people and projects more worthy of your time!

"A person starts to live when he can live outside himself."
—Albert Einstein

"There is no better feeling than helping someone you do not or never will know. I have the skill, time, and opportunity...I love doing it."
—Megan Dwyer (Age 16)
CSRA Teen Line,
Aiken County Help Line,
Aiken, South Carolina

"I enjoy meeting interesting people and helping children learn new activities."
—Bronson Rush (Age 13)
Northern Indiana Center for History,
South Bend, Indiana

CHAPTER 3

▼

SERVING THE COMMUNITY WITH PRIDE

"You must be the change you wish to see in the world."
—Mahatma Gandhi

One of the most common reasons people give for volunteering their time is a sense of duty to "give back" to their communities. Thankful for all the good things they have been given in life, many volunteers say they feel obliged to "pay it forward."

> *"Payback. We all owe debts to those we cannot thank—parents, teachers, mentors, etc. Volunteering is a way of saying thanks. It is interesting to note that the Indians didn't know who to thank for the fish in the river, so they tossed a fish back into the river as a way of saying 'thanks.'"*

> —John Kuhlman
> Manna Food Bank,
> Buncombe County Council on Aging,
> Madison County Communities in Schools,
> Foster Parents,
> Bureau of Land Management,
> New Mexico

"I have great satisfaction in knowing I can give back to society for the wonderful life I have lived in America. (I am 92 years old)."
—Sue Sherman
Arthritis Foundation,
Newton, Massachusetts

"Among those I have known, no matter where we have lived, 'giving back' has been a tradition. If people fascinate you, if you are a problem solver, and [if you are] a good listener, you volunteer."
—Norma Schlesinger
Crouse Hospital,
Syracuse, New York

For some, the impulse to give back is non-negotiable. It's a matter of principle. There are no if's, and's, or but's about it. It is something you just do.

"I enjoy giving back. It's fun and it's the right thing to do."
—Lynn Mason
University of Houston,
Big Brothers-Big Sisters,
Houston, Texas

In order for our communities and the people living in them to flourish, everybody needs to contribute their small part. It's the American way. Since volunteerism and community service was one of the key building blocks of this great nation, I strongly support the argument that it should be taught and practiced through our public schools.

"Volunteering gives me the satisfaction of peace. There is also a happy feeling deep within me knowing that I am making a difference."
—Shirley Joseph
Sickle Cell Foundation,
West Palm Beach, Florida

Fostering community is an art form that must be preserved. Why is it, then, that our public schools offer instruction in watercolor and macramé, but not on constructive ways to help build stronger communities through giving of one's time and talents? Volunteerism is every bit as much a form of self-expression as painting, speech, music, and composition. No two students will approach their volunteer projects in exactly the same way. They will always leave their individual mark on the assignments completed; with each challenge given, they will explore new avenues of kindness and ingenuity.

> *"Some people think only intellect counts; knowing how to solve problems, knowing how to get by, knowing how to identify an advantage and seize it. But the many functions of intellect are insufficient without courage, love, friendship, compassion and empathy. We care. It is our curse. It is our blessing."*
> —**Dean R. Koontz**

Just as mathematics helps develop problem-solving abilities, so too could Volunteerism 101. A student's ability to proactively address problems such as poverty and discord within communities is as fundamental to his or her development as the mastery of long division. Furthermore, classes in volunteerism, community service, and civic responsibility might go a long way in whetting kids' appetites for the study of political science—a subject about which many Americans understand far too little. One of the most important lessons America's youth should take with them from their public school educations is this:

> *"We are called to be architects of the future, not its victims."*
> —**Buckminster Fuller**

We all have the power to effect positive change; unfortunately, not all children learn this in the home. Without positive role models, how and where can we expect children from dysfunctional homes to find the tools of self-empowerment?

> *"Everyone needs to feel competent, to feel useful, to feel a sense of belonging to some group or organization, and to feel empowered to make a difference in his own life and the lives of others. Volunteering gives me all of these things."*
> —James Williams
> Indiana Youth Services Association,
> Indianapolis, Indiana

Another good reason for incorporating volunteerism into the public school curriculum is that far too many kids these days are under-socialized. When I was growing up, I spent my after-school hours playing outdoors with the neighborhood kids. For today's generation of school children, solitary activities such as surfing the Internet, playing video games, and watching television are far more common.

"Hearing children's laughter and excitement is a lot of reward by itself."

—Charles Daniels
Soccer Club,
Bartlesville, Oklahoma

Many adults fall into a similar trap. More and more, we find ourselves shopping online instead of supporting local merchants; discussing hobbies and interests in virtual chat rooms instead of at the local pubs or diners; sizing up romantic interests in a database full of photos and bios rather than at a party, church social, or from across a crowded dance floor.

"To share a smile, make the day brighter for someone less fortunate, making a difference to them. In our fast-paced schedules, we are losing the concept of giving and helping others. I believe volunteering makes a huge difference and with funding cuts, the role of my energy and time is even more critical."

—Julie McCrum
Hospice Helpline,
Area Churches Together Serving,
Aiken, South Carolina

"It's all about talking and listening... You feel good, and that shows through to everyone else."

—Liana Collalti
Freeport Memorial Hospital,
Freeport, Illinois

Isn't it ironic that, in this age of wireless communication, we as a people grow more isolated and hungry for connectivity than ever before? Human beings are pack animals. All of us crave a sense of belonging. Perhaps author John O'Donohue says it best in his book, *Eternal Echoes*:

"No one was created for isolation. When we become isolated, we are prone to being damaged; our minds lose their flexibility and natural kindness; we become vulnerable to fear and negativity."

This basic human need to connect is a strong motivating force for many who volunteer.

"It makes me feel connected to the community and as if I am making a positive change."

—Jenny Stentz
Bresee Foundation,
Los Angeles, California

"I gain a feeling of connection and hope…it's exhilarating."

—Stell Fendon
Teachers Without Borders,
Seattle, Washington

"I feel a sense of purpose, meaning, and usefulness."

—Christine Butler Mullen
The Plains Art Museum,
Fargo, North Dakota

"It really makes me feel good inside."

—Joan Marsden
United Christmas Service,
Indianapolis, Indiana

Then there is the overwhelming desire to "make a difference."

"I enjoy what I do. I know I make a difference. I do a good job and help maintain worthwhile programs. I can't imagine not volunteering."

—Marilyn Shaw
Playwrights Foundation,
San Francisco, California

"I am exhilarated to be a part of an organization that is helping our community to change, reorganize, rethink priorities. We see tangible evidence of good, empowerment, and success."

—Paula Mahone
Chrysalis Foundation,
Des Moines, Iowa

"I delight in taking a major role in successful campaigns that will result in a better and brighter future for my community."

—Sandra Volk
United Way,
American Cancer Society,
Paramount Theatre Group,
Alternatives, Inc.,
Anderson, Indiana

"I organize and keep going the Doll Squad, which cleans up donated dolls for the Samaritan Center's 'Joy Connection' store. I know every squad member beams when we stand and look at the living room couch every week after our morning's work. On it, clean dolls crowd each other, stand beside the couch, lie side by side on the rug in front of the couch. We look at each other, beam, and share satisfaction and the warm feeling that comes from a job well done— for someone else."

—June Beckett
Samaritan Center,
Ooltewah, Tennessee

Self-entitlement and greed is a pox on our society. From miserly corporate executives to the petty criminal on the street, the focus is on individual wants and needs—seldom if ever on the collective good. That's one reason why our justice system sometimes penalizes small-time offenders with community service hours rather than jail time. The hope is that, through participating in endeavors designed to benefit the community, the offender will start to identify with the people his or her actions have harmed. In the best-case scenario, offenders will find greater satisfaction in working as a force for good in their communities than they do in abusing the system for their own selfish gain.

"Until the great mass of the people shall be filled with the sense of responsibility for each other's welfare, social justice can never be attained."

—Helen Keller

"If I can show a young person…how to make wise choices in life and accept the responsibility for those choices, then I've made a difference that can help break the cycle of poverty and abuse…"

—Shawna Chapp
Rise 'n' Shine,
Seattle, Washington

One way or the other, the me-oriented society that has elevated the past-time of "looking out for number one" above even baseball and apple pie must reverse itself back in time to an age, not long ago, when Americans had a true appreciation of what's supposed to come first in life.

"Ask not what your country can do for you, ask what you can do for your country."

—President John F. Kennedy

"We must get rid of the notion that human progress rolls in on the wheels of inevitability. It comes through the tireless efforts and the persistent work of dedicated individuals, and without this hard work, time itself becomes an ally of the primitive forces of social stagnation."

—Dr. Martin Luther King, Jr.

"We sometimes feel that what we do is just a drop in the ocean, but the ocean would be less because of that missing drop."

—Mother Theresa

DID YOU KNOW?

There are tax deductions specifically designed for Americans who volunteer. Along with the standard government approved mileage rate of 14 cents per charitable mile driven, volunteers can also claim deductions for gas, oil, tolls, parking, postage, stationery, and phone calls made on behalf of their volunteer organizations.

CHAPTER 4

▼

CONNECTING WITH PEOPLE

"Walking with a friend in the dark is better than walking alone in the light."

—Helen Keller

It is said that, in order to have a friend, you must first be one. As a volunteer, the human connections you will form with people whose lives you touch are undeniable—sometimes indescribable.

"You make new friends. It gives you a new world to explore. Soon you are looking forward to those volunteer days. It will help you more than you think. It has helped me."

—Barbara Erickson
Pinellas Association for Retarded Children,
St. Petersburg, Florida

When you share the gift of literacy; when, as the reassuring voice at the end of an emergency hotline, you guide a person in crisis to safety; when your smiling face is the high point of a sick or elderly shut-in's day; the bonds you create with the people you encounter under such poignant circumstances are the type you will cherish for a lifetime.

*"We act as though comfort and luxury were the chief require-
ments of life, when all that we need to make us happy is something to be enthusiastic about."*
—Charles Kingsley

Attention singles: Quit wasting your time in the frozen-food aisle! When like-minded individuals rally around causes they are truly passionate about, fireworks often follow. Though I can't guarantee you'll meet Mr. or Ms. Right in your volunteer group, it has been known to happen. At the very least, you'll surround yourself with folks who share your goals and interests. That's the fastest way I know to expand one's circle of friends. What could be more rewarding than that?

*"There is a tremendous camaraderie with law enforcement person-
nel. There is a wonderful bonding that takes place after a period of
time. People who volunteer are some of the best, most kind and
thoughtful people one can spend time with."*
—Carol Ann Quinn
San Diego County Sheriff's Department,
Vista, California

*"Opportunities for learning and working with diverse people make
me grow and stretch. I feel a sense of belonging and doing something
worthwhile."*
—Sandra Tacke
WGBH Foundation—PBS Radio and Television,
Boston, Massachusetts

If you happen to be a youth from a small school district, the "friendship factor" of volunteerism can be especially rewarding for you. From grade school on through high school, you see the same faces in the classroom, day in and day out, year after year. Unless you become involved in sports, or other multi-school district extracurricular activities, you seldom get the chance to meet kids from other neighborhoods. Volunteerism is the ultimate extracurricular activity. It heightens your sense of compassion for others; teaches you valuable leadership skills; looks great on your college applications and resumes; and best of all, it enables you to develop friendships based on a foundation of similar values. Trust me. These are the relationships that are the most meaningful in life.

"I have met wonderful friends I will have for my lifetime through volunteering. A strong bond forms between people when you all have a cause to support."

—Patti Aresty
Morristown Memorial Hospital,
St. Hubert's Animal Welfare Center,
American Cancer Society,
Songs of Cove Foundation,
Morristown, New Jersey

The older you get, the more you come to understand that to have just one true friend in life is to be truly blessed. Sadly, it is also in old age that we face the unspeakable sadness of losing many of our dearest friends and loved ones. Withdrawing from a daily routine that has been left empty due to loss is not a healthy coping mechanism. Good memories of happier times are not enough to sustain us. We must continue to participate in life in order to live it to its fullest. From beginning to end, life is an endless cycle of redefining our priorities and reinventing ourselves.

"I am 92 years old and still in good health and want to do something for the Lord because He has been so good to me."

—Agnes Schoon
Every Child Ministries,
Hebron, Indiana

"Have you ever seen a small child's eyes get as big as plates when they discover something for the first time, or their excitement when they come up with the right answer? How about a small hand pulling on your pant leg, and when you look down you see two hopeful eyes looking up, and you hear, 'This is great, thank you!'…Rewards and feelings—indescribable and better each day. Why stay at home in my polyester pants listening to my arteries harden when I can feel young and still vital with my students by volunteering?"

—David Alexander
Waikiki Aquarium,
University of Hawaii,
Honolulu, Hawaii

"None are so old as those who have outlived enthusiasm."
—Henry David Thoreau

> *"To resist the frigidity of old age, one must combine the body, the mind, and the heart. And to keep these in parallel vigor one must exercise, study, and love."*
>
> **—Bonstettin**

Until the day we die, we are all, each and every one of us, merely works of art in progress. In this youth-oriented society, it is easy to forget that some of the most brilliant brush strokes, ones which add exciting new levels of depth and dimension, may very well come late in the artistic process. But only if we let them! We must remind ourselves that whenever a door closes, a window opens up somewhere. Volunteering can be one such window.

> *"I volunteer to help other people who need help and are not as fortunate as myself. It makes me feel good that I have helped someone in need. I get out and see how other people live and other conditions and know how fortunate I am for the things I have."*
>
> —Charlie Baddorf
> Lutheran Senior Services,
> City Fare,
> Meals on Wheels,
> Wilmington, Delaware

> *"When I stand before God at the end of my life, I would hope that I would not have a single bit of talent left and could say, 'I used everything you gave me.'"*
>
> **—Erma Bombeck**

> *"It is better to wear out than to rust out."*
>
> **—Bishop Richard Cumberland**

> *"If you associate enough with older people who do enjoy their lives, who are not stored away in any golden ghettos, you will gain a sense of continuity and of the possibility for a full life."*
>
> **—Margaret Mead**

For those who keep an open heart, volunteerism exposes us, not only to new people, but also to a different kind of love. It could be love of community; love of your fellow man; love of expressing your gratitude for a life filled with blessings; love of meeting new people and forging new relationships. How you define that love is up to you. The one thing I know for sure is that, for many, volunteerism is a sure route to finding it.

Still not convinced? Here's what some of my survey respondents had to say on the topic of making friends through volunteerism:

> *"I feel very good when I work with my volunteer organizations because they all work on bettering the world. I enjoy knowing my time is really impacting lives in the U.S. and around the world."*
>
> —Sara Green
> Leukemia and Lymphoma Society,
> Samaritan's Purse,
> North Coast Calvary Chapel,
> Carlsbad, CA

> *"I want to be active in the community, I feel I'm doing a small part to preserve animals for our planet and for my descendants. I get great satisfaction from knowing I'm doing my part to positively influence the public about issues that concern me."*
>
> —Laura Pomainville
> The National Zoo,
> Washington, DC

> *"Giving of oneself adds fulfillment and joy to life. It expands one's purpose and warms one's heart…the people one meets along the way often become valued and close friends."*
>
> —Finley Greene, Jr.
> Buffalo/Eire County Historical Museum,
> Buffalo, New York

> *"I receive many rewards from volunteering. Probably the most significant personal reward is what I learn from other people. It is a perfect network system that satisfies my curiosity and builds long-lasting friendships."*
>
> —Charlotte Wirfs
> Aurora Colony Historical Society,
> Aurora, Colorado

"The experience of working with and being around 'good people' gives me 'good karma.' When I go to bed at night, I feel as if I've lit one small candle."

—Annelle Fitzpatrick, Ph.D.
Hour Children, Inc.,
Long Island City, New York

"I meet interesting and talented people through volunteering. I gain knowledge about other people and cultures."

—Vaughn Austin
Weather Vane Community Playhouse,
Akron, Ohio

"I enjoy the interaction with the people I meet who are involved in volunteering. Without wanting to appear that I am making a broad generalization, I find the people involved are generally more interesting, more committed, and less self-absorbed."

—Nancy Seidenstein
Medical Center of Ocean County Foundation,
Brick, New Jersey

"I have made many friends, in all walks of life and of all ages, that I may not have otherwise encountered. I have learned a lot from these folks. We inspire one another and we have fun."

—Linda Lewis
Kiwanis Club of Napa,
Napa, California

"Volunteering creates balance in my life. I meet new people. I try new things. I learn new things."

—Lynn Mason
University of Houston, Big Brothers-Big Sisters,
Houston, Texas

"I love the challenge, the people I work with and for, and most of all, the feeling of accomplishment achieved."

—Jacqueline Farrington
Crouse Hospital,
Syracuse, New York

"I love the organization…the people are amazing, the energy here is infectious, and I believe in the positive power of poetry."
—Laura Bandy
Poetry Center of Chicago,
Chicago, Illinois

"Volunteering provides me with the opportunity to meet interesting, brave, and inspiring people."
—Caitlin Dugan
California Pacific Medical Center,
San Francisco, California

"I spend time and conversation with people that have similar interests. It is enlightening and exhilarating. The museum staff are fun to be with and the children on tours make comments that are delightful."
—Carol Padden
Plains Art Museum,
Fargo, North Dakota

CHAPTER 5

▼

UNIQUELY PERSONAL REWARDS

"No soul is desolate as long as there is a human being for whom it can feel trust and reverence."
                                                            —George Eliot

Some people operate under the misguided notion that volunteerism must be an act of complete selflessness. They feel that to go into it expecting a personal reward of some kind somehow diminishes the inherent goodness of the act itself. Nothing could be further from the truth! It is only natural to experience the joy of giving—for it is in giving that we receive.

"Giving of oneself is the ultimate gift—your time, your energy, your talent. I love seeing that I've made a connection with that other person through stories or hands-on. I like to feel I've made a difference."
                                                            —Annette James
                                                            Aurora Colony Museum,
                                                            Aurora, Oregon

If you think it's a myth that one can experience pure joy through giving to others, just read on and find out how it makes these volunteers feel:

"A feeling of satisfaction and of triumph...I feel so ecstatic when I see a light bulb go on in a student's eyes."

—Brandy Judkins
Literacy Volunteers of America,
Decatur, Georgia

"It is an exhilarating experience!"

—Jerry Foote
North Dakota Museum of Art,
Grand Forks, North Dakota

"It warms me, nurtures me, keeps my feet on the ground, enlivens my enjoyment of life. I've found nothing else that gives so much back to the 'giver'."

—Jackie Direen
Greater Opportunities,
San Jose, California

Often, it is the personal rewards our hearts crave that lead us to the people and organizations that need us most of all. For example, people who have beaten life-threatening illnesses are sometimes drawn to volunteer work in hospitals where they can share their survival stories with patients battling the same illness. These volunteers provide real hope and inspiration to patients and their families, and at the same time, they often find a sense of closure they didn't even know they needed. Being in the unique position to truly understand and comfort those in despair can actually help the survivor come to terms with his or her own painful experiences. It turns a negative experience into a positive one.

Volunteering can also help alleviate the terrible sense of helplessness we feel when tragedy strikes someone we love. Organizations like Mothers Against Drunk Driving (MADD) and the National Domestic Violence Hotline (NDVH), for example, allow volunteers to channel anger and grief in a way that is beneficial to others.

"I have worked at this agency four plus months now (as a full-time volunteer). I have found a peace within myself that I have not known before. I still miss my son terribly. I still walk by the beach each morning at 5:30 with my dogs and cry and speak to him as the sun rises over Lake Michigan. I still have a heavy heart 100 percent of the time. But I can see a future. My son's death was not worth the price, but it was not for nothing. It will bring some good into this

world that might not have occurred without such a tragedy. I will
not have the impact on society that David would have had, but I
will make a difference."

—Stanley Lewy
Thresholds,
Depression and Bipolar Supportive Alliance,
Chicago, Illinois

"It gives meaning to life. It's a way to fight despair and hopeless-
ness—to feel that one can do something, that fighting evil or igno-
rance is not futile. I feel empowered and purposeful."

—Annie-Louise Bennett
Survivor's Network,
Trails West, Inc.,
Council for Resource Development,
Reno, Nevada

"I am a breast cancer survivor and wish to give back to the commu-
nity through education and service, and by spreading the word
about early detection."

—Marian Lippert
Susan G. Komen Breast Cancer Foundation,
Las Vegas, Nevada

But the personal rewards we seek from volunteerism needn't stem from any-
thing particularly dramatic or life-changing. What drives us might be a passion
that needs feeding or a sense of curiosity that needs satisfying. For one nature
lover, it's as simple as:

"The scent of a marsh, the scuttle of a coot, the bray of a blue heron,
the curving creeks, the glide of a kayak."

—McCabe Coolidge
North Carolina Coastal Lana Trust,
Wilmington, North Carolina

Others are just born to teach:

"I volunteer because I love teaching children. Volunteering is not a chore but a fun activity that I really enjoy doing."
—Carolyn Rush
Boy Scouts of America,
Northern Indiana Center for History,
South Bend, Indiana

"I enjoy teaching children arts and crafts and helping people in general. By volunteering, I have met some interesting people and have learned more history."
—Jeremiah Rush (Age 19)
Northern Indiana Center for History,
South Bend, Indiana

Chances are, that docent you met the last time you visited the museum likes nothing more than being surrounded by beautiful artwork. And maybe that volunteer at the office is simply trying a new career on for size. What better way to find out about a company you are considering working for than by becoming an industrious fly on the wall? Volunteer positions sometimes evolve into full-time, paid positions. When this happens, who better to fill that paid position than an already trained, functioning member of the group dynamic?

"…the professional and social connections and the recognition that comes from taking on leadership positions are rewarding aspects of volunteering."
—Sharon Linton
Bellevue Schools Foundation,
Bellevue, Washington

"I feel an enormous sense of accomplishment and have learned an incredible number of new skills…I look forward to going to my volunteer job each day. The staff, the riders, and the volunteers have become part of my extended family."
—Patricia Diness
Winslow Therapeutic Center,
Warwick, New York

Regardless of what draws you into the volunteer lifestyle, the payback often comes in unexpected ways.

"Just to see a smile and warm embrace is worth more than any reward you can ever receive."
—Opal Perkins
St. Francis Medical Center,
Cape Girardeau, Missouri

"Volunteering at Shalimar has given me the confidence to try new things and explore and test my own capabilities and passions."
—Josh Edwards
Shalimar Learning Center,
Costa Mesa, California

DID YOU KNOW?

Some volunteer activities will actually help you achieve your fitness goals. For instance, you can burn calories while walking pound puppies or cleaning up hiking trails at a local park. It's the ultimate in multi-tasking!

Time and time again, I've heard volunteers say that nothing in this world is quite as rewarding as the feeling you get when you know that in some small way, you've helped someone.

"I know that my caring has been felt by others and that's its own reward. Friendships, laughter, and joy have enriched my life beyond description."
—Rosemary Vasseur
Gilda's Club Metro Detroit,
Royal Oak, Michigan

"I do not volunteer because I am looking for rewards, but nonetheless, I do receive things, such as joy of heart, great friends of like mind. It's educating. One builds on compassion, tolerance, acceptance of others. All these gifts make one's life more enjoyable and full of peace of heart!"
—Gregoria Zumaya
Ronald McDonald House Charities,
Reno, Nevada

*"Volunteering gives me a feeling of knowing I can make a differ-
ence. I am making a difference to those who truly need assistance.
Knowing that I'm helping make families better, particularly single-
parent families who are struggling, helps fulfill my life and helps
make it complete."*

—Gladys Onishi
Kaui Food Bank,
LiHue, Kauai, Hawaii

*"There are many good feelings that I find volunteering, but many
challenges as well. However, no matter how frustrating it can be, to
see someone's English improve, or their eyes light up when they see a
museum or hear an orchestra for the first time, or to believe that I've
truly helped someone is absolutely priceless."*

—Rodney Waters
Interfaith Ministries for Greater Houston,
Houston, Texas

*"My grandmother taught by her example and that 'We should leave
our world a better place' was a motto to share…Volunteering is not
enough, you have to give from your heart, and deeds done without
recognition have even a far greater impact. It matters that you
change another person's world positively."*

—Julie McCrum
Hospice Helpline,
Area Churches Together Serving,
Aiken, South Carolina

Word of mouth is the best form of advertising, and these folks have got me
convinced! For some it's existential, for others it's practically a form of recreation.
Beyond a shadow of a doubt, volunteerism has something good in it for everyone.
Who says the best things in life aren't free?

CHAPTER 6

▼

VOLUNTEER RESOURCES

"I find life an exciting business and most exciting when it is lived for others... True happiness is attained through loyalty to a worthy purpose."

—Helen Keller

The Internet is the best resource available for finding a volunteer opportunity that suits your interests and lifestyle. There are hundreds of Web sites out there that list volunteer openings waiting to be filled. In most cases, you simply select the category of volunteer work that appeals to you and type in your zip code. Then, voilà! You get a list of suitable volunteer organizations complete with descriptions of projects they need help with and the contact information for a volunteer coordinator who will be delighted to hear from you! The following are some of the most popular volunteerism Web sites (along with phone numbers and mailing addresses for the computer shy). Be advised that many new organizations and websites are popping up daily—so surf the Net to your heart's content. Then, once you've found the perfect fit, get up, get out, and volunteer!

Volunteer Center National Network:

Points of Light Foundation
1400 I Street, N.W. Suite 800
Washington, D.C. 20005
202-729-8000
www.pointsoflight.org

President's Call to Service:

The USA Freedom Corps
1600 Pennsylvania Avenue N.W.
Washington, D.C. 20500
1-877-USA-CORPS
www.usaFreedomcorps.gov

Literacy Project:

Reading Is Fundamental, Inc.
1825 Connecticut Avenue, N.W. Suite 400
Washington, D.C. 20009
1-877-RIF-READ
www.rif.org

National Leadership Forum:

Independent Sector
1200 Eighteenth Street, N.W. Suite 200
Washington, D.C. 20036
202-467-6100
www.independentsector.org

Online database of volunteer opportunities by zip:

VolunteerMatch
385 Grove Street
San Francisco, CA 94102
415-241-6868
www.volunteermatch.org

Resources for non-profit organizations:

Network for Good
www.networkforgood.org

Especially for leaders of volunteers:

Energize, Inc.
5450 Wissahickon Ave.
Philadelphia, PA 19144
215-438-8342
www.energizeinc.com

Volunteer management and community engagement online resource:

www.serviceleader.org

Especially for kids:

Kids Care Clubs
975 Boston Post Road
Darien, CT 06820
203-656-8052
www.kidscare.org

World Hunger Year (WHY) Kids
505 Eighth Ave., Suite 2100
New York, NY 10018-6582
212-629-8850
www.worldhungeryear.org

Earth Force
1908 Mount Vernon
Second Floor
Alexandria, VA 22301
703-299-9400
www.earthforce.org

Center for Youth as Resources
1000 Connecticut Avenue, N.W. Suite 1300
Washington, D.C. 20036
202-261-4131
www.yar.org

The Teenager's Guide to the Real World Online
www.bygpub.com/books/tg2rw/volunteer.htm

College students:

Campus Compact
Brown University
Box 1975
Providence, RI 02912
401-867-3950
www.compact.org

Service-learning/volunteerism in the schools:

National Service-Learning Clearinghouse
ETR Associates
4 Carbonero Way
Scotts Valley, CA 95066
1-866-245-SERV (7378)
www.servicelearning.org

Learn and Serve
Corporation for National and Community Service
1201 New York Avenue, N.W.
Washington, D.C. 20525
202-606-5000
www.learnandserve.org

Specifically for senior citizens:

Senior Corps
Corporation for National and Community Service
1201 New York Avenue, N.W.
Washington, D.C. 20525
202-606-5000
www.seniorcorps.org

American Association of Retired Persons (AARP)
601 E. Street N.W.
Washington, D.C.
20049
1-800-424-3410
www.aarp.org/volunteer

Virtual volunteerism:

Serviceleader.org Virtual Volunteering
www.serviceleader.org

e-Volunteerism
Energize, Inc.
5450 Wissahickon Ave.
Philadelphia, PA 19144
215-438-8342
www.e-volunteerism.com

For families who volunteer together:

National Bike Ride for the Family
www.bikerideforthefamily.org/2003/volunteer.htm

For businesses:

The Center for What Works
1001 W. Van Buren, 5th Floor
Chicago, IL 60607-2900
1-800-34-WORKS
www.whatworks.org

VolunteerMatch
385 Grove Street
San Francisco, CA 94102
415-241-6868
www.volunteermatch.org/about/corporate

To mentor a child in your area:

MENTOR/The National Mentoring Partnership
1600 Duke Street, Suite 300
Alexandria, VA 22314
703-224-2200
www.mentoring.org

Information for and about non-profit centers:

Internet Nonprofit Center
The Evergreen State Society
PO Box 20682
Seattle, WA 98102-0682
www.nonprofits.org

Other:

City Cares
600 Means Street, Suite 110
Atlanta, GA 30318
404-979-2900
www.citycares.org

Action Without Borders
79 Fifth Avenue, 17th floor
New York, NY 10003
212-843-3973
www.idealist.org

National Domestic Violence Hotline
Texas Council on Family Violence
P.O. Box 161810
Austin, TX 78716
512-794-1133
www.tcfv.org/volunteering.html

Mothers Against Drunk Driving (MADD)
MADD National Office
511 E. John Carpenter Frwy., Suite 700
Irving, TX 75062
1-800-GET-MADD (438-6233)
www.madd.org/activism

Public Sector Volunteer Opportunities
www.volunteer.gov/gov/

Servenet Volunteer Opportunities
1101 15th Street, Suite 200, NW
Washington, D.C. 20049
202-296-2992
www.servenet.org

www.ingramcontent.com/pod-product-compliance
Lightning Source LLC
Chambersburg PA
CBHW061226280526
45784CB00006B/2650